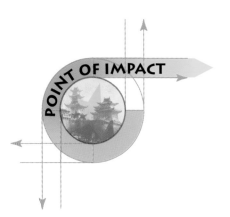

POINT OF IMPACT

The Long March

The Making of Communist China

TONY ALLAN

Heinemann Library
Chicago, Illinois

Produced for Heinemann Library by Discovery Books Limited
Designed by Ian Winton
Illustrations by Stefan Chabluk
Printed in Hong Kong

05 04 03 02 01
10 9 8 7 6 5 4 3 2 1

Library of Congress Cataloging-in-Publication Data

Allan, Tony, 1967-
   The Long March: the making of Communist China / Tony Allan.
      p. cm. -- (Point of impact)
   Includes bibliographical references and index.
   ISBN 1-58810-073-1 (lib. bdg.)
   1. China--History--Long March, 1934-1935--Juvenile literature. [1.
   China--History--Long March, 1934-1935. 2. Communism--China--History.] I. Title. II.
   Series.

   DS777.5134.A45 2001
   951.04'2--dc21   00-046086

Acknowledgments
The Publishers would like to thank the following for permission to reproduce photographs:
Peter Newark's Historical Pictures, pp. 4 and front cover (top), 9, 12, 14, 19, 27; Corbis/Brian Vikander, pp. 5 and front cover (bottom); Hulton Getty, pp. 6, 8, 10, 13, 17, 20, 21; Popperfoto, pp. 7, 22, 25, 28, 29; Corbis/Hulton Deutsch Collection, p. 11; Camera Press, pp. 15, 24, 26; Corbis/Lowell Georgia, p. 18; Hulton Deutsch Collection, p. 23.

A Note About Dates: In this book, some dates are followed by the letters B.C.E. (Before the Common Era). This is used instead of the older abbreviation B.C. (Before Christ). The date numbers are the same in both systems.

Cover photographs reproduced with permission of Corbis and Peter Newark's Historical Pictures.

Every effort has been made to contact copyright holders of any material reproduced in this book. Any omissions will be rectified in subsequent printings if notice is given to the Publisher.

Some words are shown in bold, **like this.** You can find out what they mean by looking in the glossary.

Contents

An Epic of Endurance

In the latter stages of the Long March, Red Army soldiers had to struggle up a 13,000-foot- (4,000-meter)-high pass in the Snowy Mountains. The mountain crossing was a particular ordeal for the troops, most of whom were southerners unused to ice and snow and whose quilted cotton tunics could not keep out the cold.

Crossing the Dadu River

The soldiers were already exhausted, but they were tough and battle-hardened. They were the Red Army, Chinese **Communists,** heading north after eight years of **civil war** to escape destruction by their **Nationalist** enemies. They had already traveled some 4,400 miles (7,080 kilometers) from their original base in southern China, but they still had far to go. Now the success of the entire enterprise hung on finding a crossing over the mighty Dadu River.

There were only two bridges across the river, and both were held by the enemy. The one they chose to attack was the Luding suspension bridge, an ancient structure built of massive iron chains. To take its Nationalist defenders by surprise, a regiment struck out through the mountains, covering 95 miles (153 kilometers) in 2 days.

The battle for the bridge

When they arrived, they found that the planking had been removed from their end of the bridge. So an assault force of 22 men took to the chains, swaying above the river. Some were shot, but most men struggled on to reach the planks—only to find that they had been doused in kerosene. When the defenders set the bridge on fire, the Red Army soldiers ran on through the flames, firing machine guns as they went. More troops followed. Within two hours, the Red Army had taken control of the bridge.

A fighting retreat

The capture of the Luding bridge became the most famous exploit in what was to go down in history as the Long March. Lasting a year in all, the march was a fighting retreat by the Red Army that became a daily struggle for survival. By pushing through to their goal in northern China, Communist forces lived to fight on. They reaped the reward for their efforts fourteen years later, when they finally won control of the entire country.

The "Monument to the Heroes of the People" in China's capital of Beijing honors Red Army soldiers who made the Long March between 1934 and 1935. When the Communists came to power in 1949, they celebrated the event as having forged their success and changed the fate of the nation.

VICTORY FROM DEFEAT

Communist leader Mao Zedong (also spelled Mao Tse-tung) summed up the Long March in this way: *"For twelve months we were under daily reconnaissance and bombing from the air. We were encircled, pursued, obstructed and intercepted on the ground by a force of several hundred thousand men. We encountered untold difficulties and obstacles on the way, but by keeping our two feet going we swept across a distance of more than 10,000 kilometers [6,000 miles] . . . Has there ever been a long march like ours?"*

China in Disarray

An ancient civilization

China traces its history in an unbroken line back to 1766 B.C.E.—a thousand years before the beginning of Roman civilization. Many centuries before the birth of Christ it was producing great poets and philosophers. In later eras it pioneered major technological advances long before they were known anywhere else, among them paper, printing, gunpowder, and the magnetic compass.

Beginning in 221 B.C.E., China was united under a succession of all-powerful emperors. For the most part, imperial government brought the nation unmatched levels of peace and stability. Yet by the mid-19th century, things were going terribly. The nation had began to look backwards, being fearful of change. Convinced their own ways were best, the Chinese had cut themselves off from the rest of the world, looking on foreigners as barbarians who had little to teach them. Also, those in power liked the way things were. Their interests were protected by the imperial government while the **illiterate** peasants barely made a living.

Boatmen practice their trade outside the walls of Beijing in this 19th-century engraving. By the 1830s the Chinese capital, like the nation itself, was in decline, though it still preserved the relics of its former grandeur.

The West catches up

Meanwhile, the rest of the world had been catching up. Thanks to advances made possible by the scientific revolution of the 17th century, the West had overtaken China economically and technologically. The nation that had once led the way now lagged behind the quickly-developing western world.

China's backwardness was cruelly highlighted in a series of disastrous wars. In 1842 the British, defending their opium trade in China, defeated the emperor's forces and seized Hong Kong as a British colony. Then the French took Indochina (today's Vietnam), Kampuchea, and Laos, while the Russians annexed parts of Chinese Turkestan. In 1895, the Japanese captured the island of Formosa (now called Taiwan) and forced China to give up her long-standing influence over Korea. At home discontent flared in two great rebellions, the Taiping rising of the 1850s and 1860s and the Boxer revolt in 1900. Both were put down only with the help of foreign troops. National **morale** plummeted.

A palace coup

Meanwhile, in the Chinese capital of Beijing, an imperial **concubine** seized power in a palace coup to rule as the **Dowager** Empress Ci Xi. Crushing all attempts at reform, she held onto power only with the unofficial support of the very foreign powers that had done so much to weaken China. The once-great nation's fortunes were diminishing.

Addicts are shown here in a 19th-century opium den. The drug played a central role in China's collapse. By the 1830s, as many as 12 million people were addicted to opium, which was known by many as "foreign mud." When reformers tried to ban its use, the British sent warships to protect their trade interests.

Revolution and After

Pu Yi, China's last emperor, poses in his imperial robes. Just five years old when he lost the throne, Pu Yi was allowed to remain for the next twelve years in the palace from which his ancestors had ruled the nation.

Imperial rule ends

When Ci Xi died in 1908, the next in line to be emperor, Pu Yi, was just two years old. Court-appointed **regents** governed in his stead. By then, most Chinese accepted the need for reform. The main spokesman for radical change was Sun Yat-sen (also spelled Sun Zhongshan), a doctor who had spent much of his life abroad putting forward the case for revolution in China. He got his chance in 1911, when province after province rose in revolt against the court-appointed officials who were in effect ruling the country. In February 1912, the infant emperor officially **abdicated** in favor of a new, **constitutional** republic. In so doing, he brought more than 2,000 years of imperial rule in China to an end.

But it was one thing to bring the old order down and quite another to set up a new one in its place. For all its faults, the imperial system had provided a focus for people's loyalties; with the emperor gone, there was no one to hold the nation together. Within weeks the country fell into the hands of Yuan Shikai, the former war minister, who tried unsuccessfully to make himself emperor. After his death in 1916, China fell apart.

The warlord era

The next ten years of China's history are known as the **warlord** era. Power in the country's regions fell into the hands of whoever had the strength to seize it. Usually that meant commanders in the Republican army, whose authority rested on force alone. To keep their position, they relied on the backing of soldiers they could barely afford to pay. By the end of the era, it was estimated that China had 84 separate armies with over 2 million soldiers between them, and that the cost of supporting them all would have been more than twice the national budget. In practice many simply went unpaid, living off the countryside as bandits.

In its long imperial history, China had known such periods of **anarchy** before. Now the nation waited helplessly—one system of government had gone, but as yet there was nothing to replace it.

Delegates of the **Kuomintang,** or the National People's Party, founded by Sun Yat-sen, gather in Beijing. The Nationalists were the driving force behind the revolution that swept away imperial rule in 1912.

A TIME OF HORRORS

In the chaos of the warlord years, armed gangs roamed the land. A 1929 report described how they treated civilians in one part of central China: *"When they capture a person for ransom, they first pierce his legs with iron wire and bind them together as fish are hung on a string . . . The captives are* **interrogated** *and cut with sickles to make them disclose hidden property."*

Nationalists and Communists

The rise of Chiang Kai-shek

In the chaos engulfing China, two movements sought to bring the nation back together. First and biggest were the **Nationalists,** grouped behind Sun Yat-sen's **"Kuomintang,"** or the National People's Party. After Sun's death in 1925, this fell under the control of an ambitious officer named Chiang Kai-shek.

The other group was the **Communist** Party. Inspired by the Russian Revolution of 1917, Chinese Communists looked for advice and funding from Russia, where many of them went for political and military training. There they learned the official **Marxist** philosophy, that revolution would be brought about by industrial workers in the cities. However, this seemed unlikely in China—a country that had little industry but many millions of hungry peasants.

Sun Yat-sen's successor as leader of the Nationalist movement was Chiang Kai-shek (pictured on the right). Chiang first took on the **warlords** who had divided up China between themselves. Then he began a bitter civil war against the Communists with whom he had earlier been allied.

A CLASH OF IDEAS

Although they fought a bitter 22-year **civil war,** Nationalists and Communists shared some common goals. Both wanted to see a strong, prosperous China. Nationalists sought to achieve that aim through Western-style **private enterprise.** Communists wanted to transform society from the bottom up by giving land to the peasants and by developing industry through state ownership. Within this framework, the Communist Party, rather than private individuals, would make decisions and distribute the profits.

The Northern Expedition

At first, with Russia's encouragement, Nationalists and Communists worked together to reunite the nation and defeat the warlords. Prospects looked bright in 1926 when Chiang launched his Northern Expedition, driving toward the old imperial capital of Beijing from his base in southern China. But secretly, Chiang had already decided to break with his Communist allies. He did so in dramatic fashion the following year, joining with gangsters to launch a surprise attack on striking workers in the city of Shanghai. In the fighting, thousands of people, including several Communist leaders, were killed.

Civil war breaks out

Following the Shanghai Purge, Nationalists and Communists were deadly enemies, locked in a savage civil war. At first Chiang's forces had the upper hand. Driven out of the cities, the Communists regrouped in several scattered base areas they called **"soviets."** In the prevailing **anarchy,** it was easy to dismiss them as mere bandits, little different from the other groups of lawless soldiers living off the land all over China. In fact, though, they were tightly disciplined. Toughened by their setbacks, they were biding their time.

A suspected Communist agitator is searched by military police during the Shanghai Purge of 1927. The purge was organized by Chiang Kai-shek after pro-Communist trade unions tried to seize control of the city. In all, about 5,000 Communists and their supporters were killed.

The Loss of Manchuria

The Japanese enter the picture

As if China's internal troubles were not enough, its weakness also attracted outside aggressors. The Japanese had modernized their society in the late 19th century in a way that the Chinese had failed to do. Now their military leaders looked hungrily at China's expansive territories, seeing in them a chance to solve their own overpopulation problem. Japan consisted of a series of mountainous islands, with only narrow lowland coastal regions available for people to live in.

They had already defeated China in 1895, going on to take over the kingdom of Korea. Then, after World War I, in which they backed the United States and Britain, the Japanese were rewarded with bases taken away from defeated Germany in China's northern province of Manchuria.

A recruiting poster for the Japanese army's tank corps demonstrates the militarist spirit that swept Japan in the 1930s, leading ultimately to disastrous defeat in World War II.

Crisis in Manchuria

By the start of the 1930s, the Japanese military was eager for more. In 1931 they **sabotaged** a railroad line, provoking a crisis in Manchuria that they used as an excuse to take over the whole province. The civilian government in Tokyo went along with them. They declared Manchuria to be the independent state of Manchukuo and set up Pu Yi, the boy emperor the Chinese had gotten rid of in 1912, as its **puppet ruler.** In 1933, Japanese forces went on to seize the neighboring Chinese province of Jehol.

The Japanese seizure of Manchuria was not just a blow to Chinese prestige, it was an economic disaster as well. The region was one of the country's richest. With its capture, China lost more than 40 percent of its railroads, most of its coal and iron deposits, and almost half of its export trade, as well as about a fifth of its territory.

All Chinese were shocked by this blatant assault on their homeland, but in their divided state, there was little they could do about it. Realizing that his forces were too weak to defeat the invaders, Chiang Kai-shek decided to make the best of a difficult situation by concentrating on defeating the **Communists.** *"The Japanese are a disease of the skin,"* he later declared; *"the Communists are a disease of the heart."*

Chiang's decision came at a price. Patriotic opinion was deeply offended by his failure to confront the Japanese. In the long run his half-heartedness in opposing them was to prove a costly error.

THE LAST EMPEROR

In 1932 Pu Yi, last emperor of China, was plucked from obscurity by the Japanese invaders in northern China to be puppet ruler of their newly created state of Manchukuo. Following Japan's defeat in World War II, Pu Yi lost a second throne. Imprisoned by the Communists in 1949, he was released ten years later and spent the rest of his life quietly, working as a gardener in the Beijing botanical gardens.

Japanese troops advance during their 1931 takeover of the Chinese province of Manchuria.

The Long March Begins

Communist stronghold in Jiangxi

The Japanese **incursion** came at a time when Chiang Kai-shek's **Nationalists** were tightening their grip on the Chinese nation. After the Shanghai Purge, his **Kuomintang** party established itself as the accepted government of China, though it had firm control only in the southeast. Elsewhere the **warlords** remained in charge, accepting Chiang as their leader in name only.

To most outsiders at the time, it looked like the **Communists** were through. But they had set up one sizeable **enclave** in the Jiangxi province on the borders of Chiang's southeastern stronghold. There they ruled a region of several million people, gaining the support of the peasants by introducing reforms like the redistribution of land. Dividing the land more equally was popular because it gave peasants a better chance of providing for themselves.

Mao Zedong, the future leader of the Chinese Communists, addresses an audience of peasant representatives at a 1933 conference. The 40-year-old revolutionary had risen to prominence by setting up China's largest Communist base in the Jiangxi province in the early 1930s.

A wall of fire

Chiang launched four successive attacks against the Communists in the Jiangxi **soviet,** all without success. Finally, in 1934, he threw all his resources into the Fifth **Annihilation** Campaign, encircling the soviet behind a "fiery wall" of **scorched earth** and burned villages. The plan was to starve the rebels out.

Through the spring and summer of 1934, the Communists' position grew more critical. At last, the leadership came to a desperate decision: to burst through the ring, abandoning their most important base to the enemy.

Into the unknown

The plan required absolute secrecy to have any chance of success. About 85,000 fighting men were **mobilized,** with no knowledge of where they were going. When the first units moved out on the night of October 16, they could hardly have guessed that they were setting out on an epic trek that would take them over 6,000 miles (9,650 kilometers) of some of China's roughest terrain.

Chou En-lai, shown here on horseback during the Long March, was to become Mao Zedong's most trusted adviser. After the Communist takeover of China in 1949, Chou went on to serve as the country's premier and foreign minister, becoming the leading voice for moderation in the government.

North to Shaanzi

Breaking free

The sudden departure of the **Communists** took the **Nationalist** army by surprise, and the Communist soldiers had relatively little trouble breaking through the encircling Nationalist forces. At first they headed west, hoping to join up with another **soviet** in the neighboring Hunan province. But Chiang's forces shadowed them all the way, inflicting heavy casualties and preventing them from reaching their destination.

THE GOOD TIMES

One veteran of the Long March later recalled: *"Night marching is wonderful if there is a moon and a gentle wind blowing . . . If it was a dark night and the enemy was far away, we would make torches from pine branches or frayed bamboo, and then it was truly beautiful. At the foot of a mountain, we could look up and see a long column of lights coiling like a fiery dragon up the hillside."*

This map shows the route of the Long March.

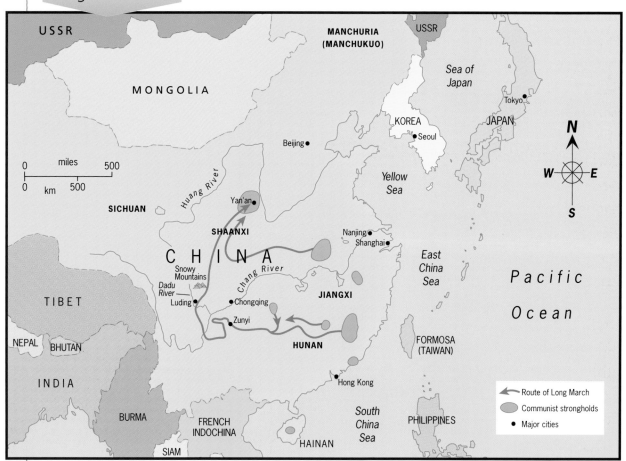

Mao to the forefront

It was at this critical point that Mao Zedong came to the forefront. The son of wealthy peasants, he had set up the Jiangxi base, only to be sidelined by people appointed by Russia who distrusted his belief in a peasant-based revolution. Now, at a conference of the Communist leadership in January 1935 in the provincial town of Zunyi, Mao's supporters brushed the Russian faction aside. From that time on Mao was to be the guiding force of Chinese Communism—a position he would hold until his death 41 years later.

Mao led his Red Army (the escaping Communist forces) west and then north through China's mountainous backbone—harsh terrain where enemy troops would have difficulty massing in force. The route he chose exposed the marchers to many hardships. Some froze to death crossing the Snowy Mountains. Others were lost in the marshy grasslands, where men sometimes had to sleep back to back on clumps of grass because there was not enough dry land to lie down upon.

Home at last

In October 1935, the tired remnants of the Red Army finally reached Shaanxi province, where they joined up with other Communist forces established there since 1930. The 85,000 who had set out had shrunk through death and **desertion** to 20,000, and they had left most of their equipment behind along the way. But they were undefeated and their **morale** was high. The Long March had let them live to fight another day.

Young volunteers line up to join the Long March toward the journey's end. While the vast bulk of those who made the journey were men, women were also welcome among the marchers, and a handful traveled the full length.

Mao's Social Experiment

An unpromising beginning

At the Long March's end, Mao and his comrades found themselves in control of a region of northeastern China so remote that only a single highway connected it to the rest of the country. Its 500,000 inhabitants were **illiterate** peasants barely producing enough food to feed themselves. There had been a terrible famine just six years earlier. Now they faced a **Nationalist** blockade and then bombing by the Japanese. For protection from air attack, Mao's soldiers began living in caves hollowed out of the soft rock of the local hills.

Today, Yan'an is a modern provincial center, but when Mao Zedong made it his headquarters in 1936, it was connected to the rest of China by only a single highway. Its remoteness made it a safe haven for the Communists, who used it as their capital for the next ten years.

Soldiers and peasants

At first sight, the new stronghold seemed unpromising territory for a social experiment, but Mao, as chairman of the Shaanxi **soviet,** set about putting his ideas for a revolutionary society into practice. **Self-sufficiency** was vital, so Red Army soldiers went to classes in sewing and weaving to learn how to make their own clothes. They worked in the fields alongside the peasants. Later, Mao would claim that the harvest doubled under **Communist** supervision. Even so, there was rarely enough food, and a typical day's diet consisted only of a few cups of barley or millet and a little cabbage. Wisely, Mao made sure the food was distributed fairly.

The other main strand of Mao's program was education. Soldiers and peasants alike learned to read and write, and there were campaigns aimed at getting rid of superstition and improving **hygiene.** A medical school and technical institutes were set up, including an academy of arts. Just as important to Mao was political **indoctrination.** Newspapers preached Communist ideas, and the Kangda military and political institute that Mao established attracted radical students from all over China. Meanwhile, he surrounded himself with a core of key supporters, most of them veterans of the march, who would in later years provide the leadership of the nation.

Telling the world

An American journalist named Edgar Snow found his way to Mao's headquarters in the town of Yan'an and wrote a book about what he saw there. *Red Star over China,* as it was titled, was an international bestseller. Mao's name became known around the world. The Communists were no longer the anonymous "red bandits" described in **Kuomintang propaganda;** they were increasingly seen as serious contenders for power, with their own radical solutions for the nation's overwhelming problems.

Shown here talking to peasants in 1939, Mao based his political strategy on organizing revolt in the countryside rather than the cities. The tactic worked well, as China had little heavy industry but many millions of poor and hungry peasants who provided the Red Army with a steady flow of new recruits.

The Struggle for China

The Japanese strike south

At first, Chiang Kai-shek was as eager to destroy the new **Communist** base in Shaanxi as he had been to demolish the Jiangxi **soviet.** But he had misjudged the mood of the nation, which was more concerned with the Japanese threat. On a trip north he was seized by a Manchurian **warlord,** who agreed to release him only in exchange for a pledge that he would link up with Mao against the invaders. So, early in 1937, the two deadly enemies found themselves unexpectedly joined as allies to save China.

The Japanese military responded quickly and brutally. From their base in Manchuria, they drove south through eastern China, the industrial and commercial heart of the nation. Beijing and Shanghai soon fell, and by the end of 1938 most major cities, including all the ports, were in their hands.

Residents of Chongqing survey the ruins of their neighborhood after a Japanese bombing raid. The Chinese had no answer to Japanese air superiority and could only bitterly assess the damage.

Retreat to the mountains

In face of the assault, the **Nationalist** armies fell back westward, as the Communists had done before them. Eventually Chiang established a new capital at Chongqing in the Sichuan province.

But even if the Japanese controlled the cities, they had difficulty policing the countryside. Mao's Communists embarked on an energetic hit-and-run campaign, employing **guerrilla tactics** to attack isolated military posts, supply convoys, and railroad lines.

THE RAPE OF NANJING

Japan's military decided to subdue the Chinese through terror. In 1937, in the **Kuomintang** capital of Nanjing, the occupying forces were let loose on the civilian population. Before the eyes of horrified foreign observers, the soldiers went on a rampage of violence, killing, and destruction. Later, an international tribunal estimated that more than 200,000 people were murdered, and many of the city's buildings were burned to the ground.

Chiang's waiting game

Meanwhile, Chiang was in Chongqing biding his time. He was sure that Japan's expansionist policies would ultimately lead it into conflict with western powers. In 1941 he was proven correct. The Japanese launched an unprovoked attack on the U.S. Navy base at Pearl Harbor in Hawaii, and the United States declared war on Japan in reply. It seemed help might be on the way at last.

An unprovoked air attack on the U.S. naval base at Pearl Harbor on December 7, 1941, brought the United States into the war against Japan. From that time on, the Chinese had a powerful ally in their struggle against the Japanese invaders.

Fight to the Finish

Brief truce

The World War II years (1941–1945) were a time of stalemate in China's internal troubles. The Japanese held onto their gains but made few further advances; they had other things on their minds. Chiang Kai-shek was playing a waiting game in Chongqing, trying to keep his armies intact to take over the country when World War II ended. The most active fighters were the **Communists,** who were still harassing the Japanese in occupied northern China.

Longtime enemies Mao and Chiang toast each other during the brief truce, arranged with American help, in early 1946. Within three months, Communists and Nationalists were at war again, this time in a fight to the finish.

The frail truce between Chiang and Mao broke down early in 1941, and from then on **Nationalists** and Communists were once more at each other's throats. But that situation changed again with the Japanese surrender in August 1945. The United States and the **Soviet Union**—the two victorious Allies with direct interests in China—both had their own reasons for wanting to see the country united. So in January 1946, despite their personal differences, Chiang and Mao were once more persuaded to join forces briefly.

War to the bitter end

However, their differences went too deep to be set aside lightly. Within three months the two sides were back at war, and there would be no more truces.

At the time, the Nationalists seemed to have the advantage. Their armies numbered 3.7 million men in 1945, and they had more than 1,000 U.S.-supplied planes. Against them the Communists could muster less than a tenth of that force, and only half their soldiers were armed at all.

In addition, Chiang could count on extensive financial assistance from the United States—more than 2 billion dollars between 1945 and 1949—while Mao received little from a Soviet Union itself weakened by war. With the Japanese withdrawal, the Nationalists also regained control of the nation's major cities and industries. Many thought that it was only a matter of time before Chiang would destroy the Communists and reunite the nation. But appearances were deceptive—events were to prove them terribly wrong.

Street vendors sell flags of the victorious allies to Shanghai residents celebrating the Japanese surrender at the end of World War II. The removal of the Japanese threat promised a new dawn for China, and for a time there was hope that all parties would work together to create a democratic future.

The Nationalist Debacle

Corruption weakens the army

Nationalist fortunes in the **civil war** reached a high point early in 1947. For a time Chiang's forces controlled every provincial capital in China; they even managed to drive Mao from his long-established base in Yan'an. But soon things started to go wrong.

In fact the problems began much earlier, in the years of enforced idleness in Sichuan. Corruption harmed the Nationalist war effort. While the officers lived on funds from foreign aid and taxes, the peasant soldiers often went unpaid. **Morale** was disastrously low; new recruits often had to be roped together to keep them from **deserting.** As for the Sichuanese themselves, they referred to Chiang's army as "downriver bandits."

The curse of inflation

At the end of World War II, a new problem further undermined the Nationalist cause: inflation. To pay its way, Chiang's government had printed more and more money, which steadily

Red Army troops advance in the course of the crucial 1948 campaign that gave them control of northeastern China. In the fighting, Chiang Kai-shek lost his best troops, which were cut off from their fellow Nationalist forces in the south and forced to surrender.

lowered the value of the currency. By 1948, the situation had spiraled out of control and prices went through the roof. In 1937, a farmer with 100 Chinese dollars could purchase 2 oxen, but by 1949, the same amount would buy just a sheet of paper! In 1948, the cost of rice, the nation's main food, could go up six times in one day. People's savings became worthless, and starvation spread throughout the streets of the cities.

With their policy of **self-sufficiency,** Mao's troops were hardly touched by the problems of inflation; they were used to living off the land and had little need for money. Now they found that Nationalist troops, paid in worthless paper, were only too willing to sell them their guns for a few handfuls of grain.

Now the Red Army swept across northern China, first cutting off some of Chiang's best troops in Manchuria and then disarming them. By mid-1948, they found that whole divisions were coming over to them; three-quarters of all the soldiers they captured gave up without a fight. By that autumn, the situation had reversed. Now it was the **Communists** who had the men and the weapons—the remaining Nationalists were on the run and fighting for their lives.

Looting breaks out in the streets of Nanjing in the panicky days before Communist forces moved into the city. The Nationalist capital finally fell in April 1949.

RULES OF CONDUCT

The Communists imposed strict discipline over their soldiers, as this Red Army marching song shows:

> *Speak politely.*
> *Pay fairly for what you buy.*
> *Return everything you borrow.*
> *Pay for any damage.*
> *Don't strike or swear at people.*
> *Don't damage the crops.*
> *Don't take liberties with women.*
> *Don't mistreat captives.*

The Final Showdown

China "lost" to the Communists

The outside world watched in amazement as Chiang Kai-shek's armies disintegrated around him. For many years afterwards, U.S. politicians would argue over who "lost" China to the **Communists.** In fact, the **Nationalist** forces largely self-destructed; Chiang paid the penalty for being too dependent on the cities and out of touch with the peasants who made up the bulk of China's 600 million people.

Chiang goes to Taiwan

The end came quickly. The last great battle of the **civil war** was fought from late 1948 on, around the Nationalist capital of Nanjing. The city fell in April

Red Army forces enter the old imperial capital of Beijing in January 1949. The troops were greeted as liberators and encountered no resistance there.

1949, though Chiang Kai-shek had already retreated—first south to Canton, then west to Sichuan, where he had sought refuge from the Japanese eleven years earlier. This time, though, he had no serious hope of regaining lost ground. Eventually he left with the remnants of his followers for the island of Formosa, now called Taiwan, in the East China Sea. There he set up the Republic of China, ruling over what he saw as a **government in exile,** ready to take control over mainland China should the political situation ever permit. His successors remain in control of Taiwan to this day.

The birth of the People's Republic

On the mainland, the victors took their time to establish control over their vast dominions. It was October 1, 1949, when Mao finally proclaimed the People's Republic of China before one million people in Beijing's Tiananmen Square, where the advent of new dynasties had been formally proclaimed in imperial times. The note he struck in his speech was one of national pride. *"Ours will no longer be a nation subject to insult and humiliation,"* he proclaimed. *"We have stood up."* After 22 years of civil war and invasion and more than a century of national decline, he told the nation what it long had been waiting to hear.

在毛澤東的勝利旗幟下前進

This **propaganda** poster shows soldiers and civilians alike saluting the triumph of the Communist Party and its leader, Mao Zedong.

The March's Long Shadow

Mao the social visionary

The **Communist** victory in 1949 put China in the hands of veterans of the Long March. Their exploits became part of national legend, and every Chinese schoolchild learned of heroic feats like the capture of the Luding bridge. The new rulers carried over into their system of government something of the spirit of the march itself. In power, they were as tough on corruption and greed as they had been on looting and lack of discipline among the troops.

Soldiers recite from the *Thoughts of Chairman Mao,* contained in a "little red book." No criticism of Mao's views was permitted for, as the book itself stated, *"Not to have a correct political point of view is like having no soul."*

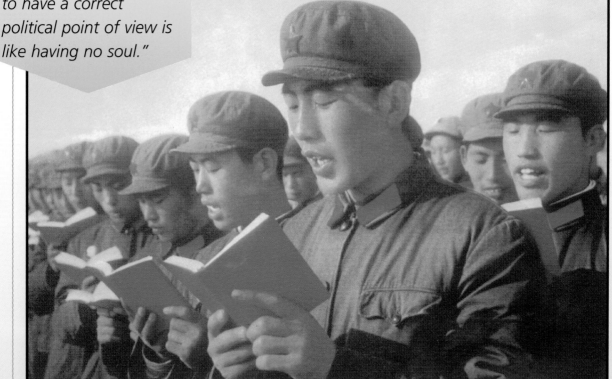

Yet there was to be no happy ending for the march's leaders themselves. Under the new government, power became increasingly concentrated in the hands of one man, Chairman Mao, a social visionary with a determination to put his ideas into practice whatever the cost. Never tolerant of criticism, Mao grew increasingly suspicious of his old comrades-in-arms, whom he came to suspect of plotting against him.

Cultural Revolution—a time of suffering

The climax came in the Cultural Revolution, a mass movement engineered by Mao in the mid-1960s to encourage what he called "continuous revolution" in Chinese society. At its height, fanatical Red Guards fanned out across the nation in a quest to root out the "Four Olds"—old culture, old ideas, old customs, and old habits. Politically, their main targets were the very leaders who had marched and fought with Mao so long ago. Some were driven from office, others were publicly humiliated or even killed.

Red Guards force suspected political opponents to wear dunce's caps in Beijing during the Cultural Revolution of the late 1960s. Those considered guilty of not following the Maoist party line were subjected to physical violence as well as public humiliation. It was later estimated that about 35,000 died as a result.

Mao's successor

Yet one did survive. Deng Xiaoping had a relatively minor role in the march itself, but later rose high in the Communist hierarchy. His family was physically attacked in the Cultural Revolution—his son was left paralyzed from the waist down, and he himself was sent to work in a tractor factory. But he managed to win his way back into favor, and when Mao finally died in 1976, it was he who won the power struggle to succeed him.

Deng remained in charge until his own death in 1997, at the age of 93. Thus, even six decades after it finished, the Long March continued to cast its shadow over Chinese life, providing the nation's leadership up to the threshold of the new millennium.

Important Dates

1912		Last **emperor abdicates.** End of imperial rule.
1916		Start of **warlord** era
1924		**Nationalist Kuomintang** party admits **Communists** as members
1925		Death of Sun Yat-sen, the "father of the Chinese Revolution"
1926		Chiang Kai-shek launches Northern Expedition against warlords
1927		Chiang launches Shanghai Purge of Communists
1928		Kuomintang forces capture Beijing from warlords
1930		Chiang's First **Annihilation** Campaign against Communists
1931		Japanese forces occupy Manchuria
1933		Fifth Annihilation Campaign launched
1934	**October**	Long March begins
1935	**January**	Mao elected Communist Party Chairman at Zunyi
	May	Luding suspension bridge over Dadu River captured
	October	Long March ends in Shaanxi province
1936	**January**	Communists set up capital at Yan'an
	December	Warlord revolt forces Chiang into alliance with Mao
1937		Japanese forces invade southern China. Rape of Nanjing.
1938		Chiang retreats from Japanese, westwards to Sichuan
1941	**January**	Nationalists and Communists break their truce
	December	Japanese attack Pearl Harbor
		United States declares war on Japan
1945		World War II ends
		Japan, defeated, withdraws from China
1946		Full-scale civil war resumes between Nationalists and Communists
1946	**March**	Nationalists capture Communist capital of Yan'an
	December	Nationalist forces defeated in Manchuria
1948		Hyper-inflation undermines Nationalist war effort
1949	**January**	Beijing falls to Communists
	October	Mao proclaims the People's Republic of China
	December	Nationalists complete withdrawal to Formosa (now called Taiwan)
1950	**October**	China invades Tibet
	November	Chinese forces intervene in Korean War
1966		Mao inaugurates the Cultural Revolution
1976		Death of Chairman Mao. Deng Xiaoping succeeds him as leader.
1997		Death of Deng Xiaoping

Glossary

abdicate to give up power or step down from the throne

anarchy condition of lawlessness

annihilation total destruction

civil war war between different groups within the same country

Communist someone who believes that the state, not individual people, should own all important industry, property, and wealth

concubine secondary wife in societies where more than one wife is allowed

constitutional adhering to an established written framework

desertion willful abandonment of a military post

dowager wealthy widow

enclave district surrounded by foreign or hostile territory

government in exile ruling body forced from its native land that hopes one day to return

guerrilla tactics method of warfare usually involving harassment and sabotage

hygiene principles of cleanliness and good sanitation to improve health

illiterate unable to read or write

incursion raid in hostile territory

indoctrination thought control; forced education in ideas that are not allowed to be criticized

interrogate to question closely, often under threat of force

Kuomintang Chinese Nationalist party set up by Sun Yat-sen

Marxist reflecting the views of Karl Marx, founder of the international Communist movement

mobilize to prepare an army for action

morale good feeling that a group of people has about itself

Nationalist in China, a follower of the republican movement led first by Sun Yat-sen and then Chiang Kai-shek

private enterprise companies owned and operated by individuals and not by the state

propaganda misleading information meant to persuade people to adopt a certain viewpoint

puppet ruler ruler in name only, manipulated by others

reconaissance watching the enemy to discover their position and the condition of their troops

regent someone who rules a country when the king or queen is too young or unable to do so

sabotaged secretly destroyed buildings and machinery

scorched-earth wartime policy of destroying anything that may be useful to the enemy

self-sufficiency lifestyle allowing people to support themselves without the help of others

soviet in China, an area governed along Communist lines

Soviet Union huge Communist country, including Russia, that broke up in the 1990s into separate countries

warlord ruler kept in power by military strength alone

More Books to Read

Dramer, Kim. *People's Republic of China*. Danbury, Conn.: Children's Press, 1999.

Stefoff, Rebecca. *Mao Zedong: Founder of the People's Republic of China*. Brookfield, Conn.: Millbrook Press, Inc., 1996.

Thomas, Graham. *Timeline: People's Republic of China*. North Pomfret, Vt.: Trafalgar Square, 1990.

Index